D1064673

How to Write a Biography

by Cecilia Minden
and Kate Roth

CHERRY LAKE PUBLISHING · ANN ARBOR, MICHIGAN

Published in the United States of America by Cherry Lake Publishing
Ann Arbor, Michigan
www.cherrylakepublishing.com

Content Adviser: Gail Dickinson, PhD, Associate Professor, Old Dominion
University, Norfolk, Virginia

Photo Credits: Page 4, ©Catalin Petolea/Shutterstock, Inc.; page 14,
©Rtimages/Shutterstock, Inc.; page 17, ©iStockphoto.com/ManoAfrica;
page 18, ©Jonathan Ross/Dreamstime.com; page 21, ©Kate Roth

Library of Congress Cataloging-in-Publication Data
Minden, Cecilia.
  How to write a biography / by Cecilia Minden and Kate Roth.
      p. cm. — (Language arts explorer junior)
  Includes bibliographical references and index.
  ISBN 978-1-61080-491-2 (lib. bdg.) — ISBN 978-1-61080-578-0
  (e-book) — ISBN 978-1-61080-665-7 (pbk.)
  1. Biography as a literary form—Juvenile literature. I. Roth, Kate. II. Title.
  CT22.M56 2012
  920—dc23   2012008167

Cherry Lake Publishing would like to acknowledge the work
of The Partnership for 21st Century Skills. Please visit
www.21stcenturyskills.org for more information.

Printed in the United States of America
Corporate Graphics Inc.
July 2012
CLFA11

Table of Contents

CHAPTER ONE

What a Life!

A good biography can be just as exciting as a made-up story.

Have you ever read a biography? Biographies help us learn about the lives of real people. They can be about famous people, such as sports stars, artists, or world leaders. They can also be about regular people. Everyone has a story to tell.

You can write a biography about someone you know!

Here is what you will need to complete the
activities in this book:

- Blank notebook paper
- Pencil with an eraser
- A computer (optional)

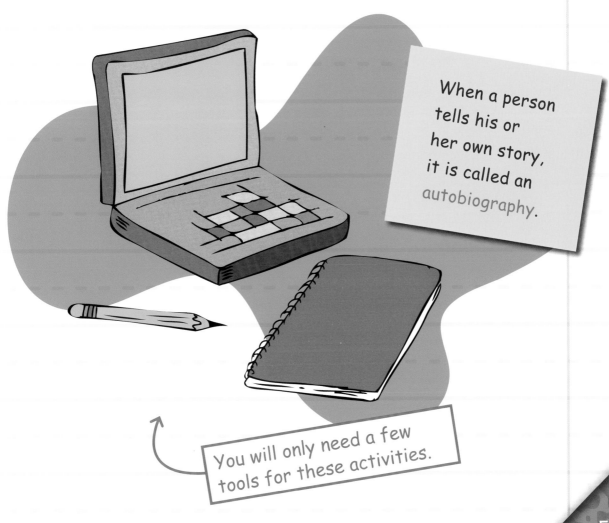

When a person
tells his or
her own story,
it is called an
autobiography.

You will only need a few
tools for these activities.

CHAPTER TWO

Write About Anyone!

You can write a biography about anyone!

Whom do you want to write about? The subject of your biography does not have to be famous. He or she does not even have to be an adult. Think about the people in your life. You might want to learn more about a friend, coach, grandparent, neighbor, or person at your school. Pick someone of interest to you. You may be surprised by what you learn about the people you see every day!

Begin by making a list of people you could write about. Write down all of your ideas. You will do **research** to learn more about one of these people. Who has the story you would like to write?

Make a List

In this activity, you will make a list of possible subjects for your biography.

INSTRUCTIONS:
1. Make a list of possible subjects for your biography.
2. Choose someone who is interesting to you.

Subjects for My Biography
- Uncle John, a war hero
- My neighbor Jack, the drummer in his college band
- Grandma Sally, a great cook
- My friend Annabel, who lives in China

You need to do research to write a good biography.

To get a copy of this activity, visit www.cherrylakepublishing.com/activities.

CHAPTER THREE

What Do You Want to Know?

Once you decide who to write about, you can decide what you want to learn about him or her. You will need to do research to learn about your subject. Sometimes you can do research from a book or on the computer. For this biography, you will do research to learn about your subject with an **interview**.

Make a list of what you already know about this person. Don't write down a fact about someone unless you are completely sure it is true. Then make a list of what you would like to know. You can make a list of questions from this second list.

Your first questions should help you find out where and when the person was born. Next, write questions about what it was like when she was growing up. How was her life different from yours? Write questions about what she liked to do. What kinds of places did she like to visit?

If the person is older, you can move on to questions about her life as an adult. What are her greatest **accomplishments**? What are the most important things about her life that she wants others to know?

What can you find out that will be of special interest to your readers? The purpose of your interview is to find out what makes your subject interesting.

To get a copy of this activity, visit www.cherrylakepublishing.com/activities.

ACTIVITY

Prepare to Interview Your Subject

In this activity, you will prepare the questions for your interview.

INSTRUCTIONS:
1. Write the title "What I Know" at the top of the page.
2. Below the title, write facts you already know about your subject's life.
3. On a second page, write the title "What I Want to Know."
4. Below the title, write what you want to learn from the interview.
5. On a third sheet of paper, write your ideas for questions to ask your subject. Your notes about what you want to learn can help you think of questions.
6. Leave space under each question to write down the person's answers.

My friend, Annabel

What I Know:

- 10 years old
- 5 people in her family
- Lived in the United States and China
- Likes to travel
- Enjoys scuba diving and everything about the ocean

What I Want to Know:

- What does Annabel like most about living in China?
- What does she miss the most about the United States?
- Where are her favorite places to travel?
- What does she want to be when she grows up?

Questions:

- Where and when were you born?
- Can you tell me a little about your family?
- What do you miss about the United States?
- What is your favorite thing about living in China?
- Where are some of your favorite places to travel?
- What do you want to be when you grow up?
- Where do you want to live when you grow up?

CHAPTER FOUR

Questions and Answers

Call or write the person to set up a time for your interview. Make sure you set aside plenty of time to ask your questions. You don't want to rush the interview. It is a good idea to use a **recorder** during the interview. That way you can check your information when you are writing. Ask for permission before recording the interview.

Look at the person while he is talking. Be a good listener. Follow your list of questions. Other questions may come up during the interview. Keep good notes on what was said.

Ask if you may record the interview.

To get a copy of this activity, visit www.cherrylakepublishing.com/activities.

ACTIVITY

Interview Your Subject

In this activity, you will interview the subject of your biography.

INSTRUCTIONS:

1. Turn on the recorder if you are using one. Don't forget to turn it off after the interview.
2. Ask the questions on your list. Give the speaker time to answer each one.
3. Listen carefully. Take notes on what you want to remember about each answer. Your notes do not have to be full sentences, but they should be clear so you can understand them later.
4. Look at the speaker as you ask your questions.
5. After the interview, thank the person for taking time to talk with you.

> Always use good manners and be polite during an interview.

Q. Where were you born?
A. Massachusetts, in the United States

Q. Tell me a little about your family.
A. • 5 people: mom, dad, younger brother and sister
   • 4 grandparents and great grandpa (age 95)

Q. What do you miss about the United States?
A. The food! Strawberries from local farms

CHAPTER FIVE

Organize Your Information

It will be easier to write your biography if you organize your notes before you start.

Now you are ready to write a **draft** of your biography. Choose which information you want to use from your notes. You do not have to use everything you learned. Think about what **adjectives** you can use to describe this person and her life. Write what is important or interesting about your subject. What makes her unique? Help the reader see the person as you do.

Biographies are often written in **chronological** order. This means you write events in the order they happened. You should also organize the information into **categories**. Categories are sections with information on one topic. For example, your first category might be the subject of growing up. Next, you write about events in the person's life. Finally, you write about the person's special accomplishments.

Use **quotations** from your interview. When you quote someone, you must write exactly what he or she said. Using quotations will allow your readers to hear your subject's voice.

Create a Draft

In this activity, you will write a draft of your biography.

INSTRUCTIONS:
1. Choose the information you want to use from your research.
2. Write an opening statement to grab the reader's attention. For example, use an interesting quotation from your subject.
3. Put the information in chronological order.
4. Divide the information into two or three categories. Each category will form a **paragraph** in the body of the biography.
5. Write a closing comment that includes a summary of your subject's life.
6. Add any quotations to your report. Be sure to use quotation marks.

Remember to put quotation marks around the person's exact words.

To get a copy of this activity, visit www.cherrylakepublishing.com/activities.

May I Present . . . ?

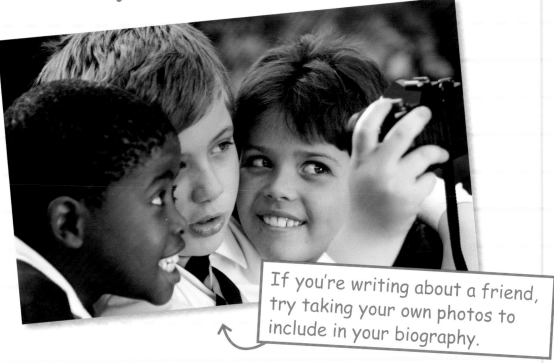

If you're writing about a friend, try taking your own photos to include in your biography.

After you finish your draft, go over your work. Make changes until everything is just right. Add a title to your biography. Write your final copy on a blank sheet of paper or type it using a computer.

Biographies often contain pictures of the subject. Find photographs or draw illustrations to go with your writing.

Write the Final Copy

In this activity you will write the final copy of your biography.

INSTRUCTIONS:
1. Write the final copy of your biography on a blank sheet of paper or type it on a computer.
2. Add photographs or drawings of your subject so your readers can see the person throughout his or her life.

Family photo albums are a great place to find pictures for your biography.

To get a copy of this activity, visit www.cherrylakepublishing.com/activities.

ACTIVITY

Final Changes

Check everything one more time.

☐ YES ☐ NO Do I have a title and opening that will grab the reader's attention?

☐ YES ☐ NO Do I help the reader get to know the biography's subject?

☐ YES ☐ NO Do I use words that explain the chronology of events?

☐ YES ☐ NO Do I include details that help give the reader a clearer picture of the person?

☐ YES ☐ NO Is the information organized into categories with headings?

☐ YES ☐ NO Do I have an illustration or photograph of the subject?

☐ YES ☐ NO Do I include a quotation from the person?

☐ YES ☐ NO Do I include a summary in my ending?

☐ YES ☐ NO Do I use correct grammar and spelling?

Share your biography with your subject and with others. Let others learn about this unique life!

Adventurous Annabel

INTRODUCTION

Annabel Roth is adventurous. Even though she is only 10 years old, she has been to more places than many adults. She has had quite a life!

Annabel was born in Massachusetts, America. Annabel was the first child, grandchild, and niece in her family. When she was born, everyone wanted to meet her.

FAMILY AND HOME LIFE

Annabel has 5 people in her family including her mom and dad; younger brother, Andrew; and little sister, Alexandria. She has 4 grandparents and a great-grandpa who is 95 years old. Annabel lived in America until she was 7, and then she moved to China. She speaks English at home and Mandarin at school. One of Annabel's first memories of China was when her family's couch was delivered on the back of two bicycles. "There are bikes everywhere in China," she said. Annabel likes living in China but misses America, too. She said, "I really loved eating strawberries from a local farm in America."

FAVORITE ACTIVITIES

Annabel loves to travel with her family. She has been to 15 countries on 5 continents. One of her favorite trips was to Cambodia. She loved watching the sunrise on the ancient temple named Angkor Wat. She has held pandas in China and ridden elephants in Thailand. In Australia she rescued a wild kookaburra bird. "You have to be brave when you travel. You never know what amazing things will happen. I try to bring my camera everywhere."

WHEN SHE GROWS UP

Annabel wants to be a marine biologist when she grows up. She wants this career because she likes the ocean, and she wants to be a scientist. She has been scuba diving one time. She said, "Scuba diving was scary and fun, but I want to get better so I can learn a lot about the ocean." She would like to live all over the world. "Every country has something interesting."

ANNABEL'S FURTHER ADVENTURES

I think my friend Annabel has had a very interesting life and has many exciting adventures ahead of her. I plan to join her on many of them!

Glossary

accomplishments (uh-KAHMP-lish-muhnts) important things a person has done in his or her life

adjectives (AD-jik-tivz) words used to describe nouns

autobiography (aw-toh-bye-AH-gruh-fee) a book in which the author tells the story of his or her own life

biography (bye-AH-gruh-fee) a book telling the story of a person's life

categories (KAT-uh-gor-eez) similar ideas grouped together

chronological (krah-nuh-LAH-ji-kuhl) arranged in the order in which events happened

draft (DRAFT) an early version of a written document

interview (IN-tur-vyoo) a meeting during which a person is asked questions

paragraph (PARE-uh-graf) a group of sentences about a certain idea or subject

quotations (kwoh-TAY-shuhnz) sentences or short passages that are written or spoken by one person and repeated by another

recorder (ri-KOR-dur) a device for recording sounds to play back later

research (REE-surch) a study or investigation into a particular subject

For More Information

BOOK

Fletcher, Ralph. *How to Write Your Life Story*. New York: Collins, 2007.

WEB SITE

Ralph Fletcher

www.ralphfletcher.com/tips.html

Get some great writing tips from a famous author!

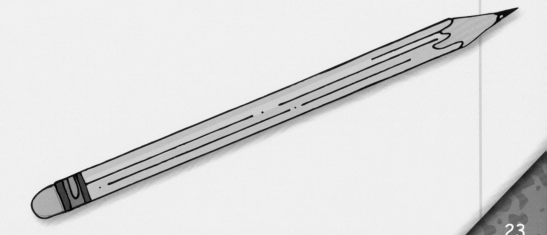

Index

About the Authors

Cecilia Minden, PhD, is the former director of the Language and Literacy Program at Harvard Graduate School of Education. She earned her doctorate from the University of Virginia. While at Harvard, Dr. Minden also taught several writing courses. Her research focused on early literacy skills and developing phonics curricula. She is now an educational consultant and the author of more than 100 books for children. Dr. Minden lives with her family in Chapel Hill, North Carolina. She likes to write early in the morning while the house is still quiet.

Kate Roth has a doctorate from Harvard University in language and literacy and a master's from Columbia University Teachers College in curriculum and teaching. Her work focuses on writing instruction in the primary grades. She has taught first grade, kindergarten, and Reading Recovery. She has also instructed hundreds of teachers from around the world in early literacy practices. She lives in Shanghai, China, with her husband and three children, ages 3, 7, and 10. Her oldest two children, Annabel and Andrew, worked together to write the example used in this book.